Another Chance

-

Jack's Curated Business Idea

-

Jack Lookman

Another Chance - Jack's Curated Business Idea

Copyright © 2024 Jack Lookman Limited and Olayinka Carew aka Jack Lookman

All rights reserved.
No portion of this book may be reproduced in whole or in part, in any form or by any means, electronic or mechanical including photocopying, recording, or by any information storage and retrieval system, without the consent and written permission from the copyright owners, individually or collectively.

CONTENT :

CONTENT :	3
A. Acknowledgement	8
B. Dedication	9
C. About the book	10
D. Aims of the project	11
E. Connect With Us	12
F. Preamble	13
G. The Collection	15
H. Target Audience	16
I. Polite request:	17
Another Chance	18
1. What's the inspiration for this project?	18
2. What's the Idea?	18
3. What are the Benefits?	19
3.1 To the entrepreneur:	19
3.2 To Society:	19
3.3 To the user:	19
3.4 To Government:	20
4. Business Name and URL	20
5. Business Registration and Ownership	21
6. Could I collaborate?	21
7. Digital Footprints	21
8. Marketing Plan	22
9. Search Engine Optimization and Keyword Research	23
10. Niche, Demographics, and Client Avatar	24
11. Format	24
12. Mission	24
Our mission is to empower and inspire generations by leveraging the internet.	24

13. Curriculum and Signposts	24
14. Disclaimer and Indemnifications	26
15. Target audience	27
16. Content Creation Implementation	27
17. Language	28
18. Outsourcing	28
18.1 Some of the freelancing platforms you may consider are:	29
19. The Value Proposition	29
20. Could there be a Sales funnel?	30
21. Will Payment be one-off or Recurring?	31
22. Funding Options	31
23. Sponsorships	32
24. Income Streams	32
25. Prioritization	33
26. Costing and Pricing Considerations	33
27. Research and Development	34
28. Complimentary Products and Services	35
29. Budgetary Considerations	35
30. Will there be certifications for students?	35
31. What problem are you solving?	36
32. Legalities	37
33. Platforms	37
34. Risk Management Considerations	37
35. Expectation Management	38
36. Profit-Sharing Formula	38
37. Business Plan	39
38. Must All the Content Be Mine?	40
39. Is there a need for Feedback Mechanisms?	40
40. Skills Required for the Business	41
41. Could the business be automated?	41

42. How much is required to start the business?	42
42.1 Some of the key milestones are:	42
43. Funding	42
44. How Soon Could the Business be Up and Running?	43
45. How do I go About Starting the Business?	43
46. Do I need to be an Expert?	44
47. Could Passive Residual Income be Earned from this Business?	44
48. Unique Selling Proposition	45
49. Resources Required for The Business	45
50. Requirements For the Client	45
51. Should the product be Local or Global?	46
52. Process and Project Management	46
53. Do I Require an Office for This Business?	47
54. Benefits And Opportunities	47
55. Threats and Weaknesses	48
56. Could the Products and Services become Evergreen?	48
57. Monetization Plan	49
58. Value	51
A. Useful links:	53
B. About Jack Lookman	55
C. Important Notice:	56
D. Feedback	56
E. Signposts:	56
F. Disclaimer	57
G. Mission	57
H. Did you get value?	57
I. Useful compliments	59
J. Useful hashtags	60
K. Books by Jack Lookman	60
L. Some resources by Jack Lookman	61

M. Will you like to collaborate?	62
N. Will you like to be mentored by Jack Lookman?	62
O. OTHER PUBLICATIONS BY Jack Lookman Limited	62

A. Acknowledgement

John Tosin Adekunle is acknowledged for his contribution to this project.

My parents, siblings, children, teachers and others, who have contributed to my being, are much appreciated.

My Creator and Sustainer is glorified, for seeing me through different facets of my being.

Alhamdu lillahi rabbi alAAalameena.

To God be the glory.

B. Dedication

This piece of work is dedicated to all Entrepreneurs and Entrepreneurial minds throughout the world.

C. About the book

This book is one of many in the series, 'Jack's Curated Business Ideas.'

In my native Yoruba language, there's a saying that 'some have a head, without a cap,' and vice versa.

This project is an attempt to share many viable business ideas, to enable interested parties to execute.

If consultancy or collaboration is required, we shall be glad to offer these.

Audio versions could be found on Social media:

- Youtube
- Facebook
- TikTok
- Jack's Empowerment - jacksempowerment.com
- Etc

D. Aims of the project

- To share viable Curated Business Ideas
- To empowering and inspiring generations
- To add societal value
- To reduce unemployment
- To monetize
- To create wealth
- To reduce crime
- Etc

E. Connect With Us

Facebook group: Curated Business Ideas

Youtube channel: Curated Business Ideas

Facebook Community - Jack Lookman

TikTok - Jack Lookman

LinkedIn - Olayinka Carew aka Jack Lookman

Jack's Empowerment: jacksempowerment.com

Curated Business Ideas - curatedbusinessideas.com

F. Preamble

Quite a number of people have missed out of education for one reason or the other.

Do they deserve a second chance?

Do they deserve another chance?

If they become empowered and inspired...

Could they become assets to themselves?

Could they become assets to society?

Could they add immense value to society?

Should we leave them to their devices?

Should we just look away?

And pretend it has nothing to do with us?

Should we look on, and let society degenerate?

Or should we act, within our ways and means?

This book is Jack Lookman's effort, at contributing in his little way, to impact society and humanity.

Have a great and insightful read.

Best wishes

Jack Lookman

G. The Collection

We have quite a number of books on Jack's Curated Business Ideas.

Please visit jacklookmanlimited.com for the full list of paperbacks.

We shall also be uploading the content to our blog: curatedbusinessideas.com

You could find the videos on our Social media platforms:

Youtube channel - Curated Business Ideas

Facebook group: Curated Business Ideas

The videos could also be found on our membership site: jacksempowerment.com

H. Target Audience

- Entrepreneurial minds
- Entrepreneurial educators
- Marginalized people
- Those seeking opportunities
- Etc

I. Polite request:

- Take notes
- Capture any latent creative ideas that may come your way
- Take action
- Leverage similar minds
- Monetize
- Make impact
- Leave a great legacy
- Consult with Jack Lookman as necessary
- Spread the word
- Become an Ambassador to the Jack Lookman brand
- Check out other content by Jack Lookman

Hello, greetings to one and all, this is Jack Lookman welcoming you to our series, Jack's Curated Business Ideas. Today's topic is

Another Chance

Just a short announcement; the full video could be found on our YouTube channel which is 'Curated Business Ideas.' It shall also be timestamped just for ease of reference; the book could be purchased on Amazon amazon.co.uk

You could also find the content on our blog which is curatedbusinessideas.com and this shall also be from June 2024 by God's grace.

1. What's the inspiration for this project?

An acquaintance was introduced to me by a friend; he apparently got into trouble at a young age. He therefore spent a long while in incarceration. Upon his exit or discharge, rather than becoming a troublemaker and a nuisance, he decided to spend time being constructive, making notes of slacks in the system and working at making amends and adding value to one and all; to himself and to society.

2. What's the Idea?

Upon having different sessions with him, the idea crossed my mind to create content that could benefit those in similar situations; it could add value to them, by teaching them in cost-effective and easy-to-understand ways. They could also be realigned with the society. They could add value to themselves as well as to society. They could become role models. They could erase their past and rewrite their future. They could do their learning at their own pace and in language or languages of choice.

3. What are the Benefits?

3.1 To the entrepreneur:

- Monetization
- Making impact
- Wealth creation
- Job creation
- etc.

3.2 To Society:

- Reduced crime
- Added societal value
- Easier reintegration
- Reduced cost of governance
- etc.

3.3 To the user:

- Affordable and flexible training and development
- Job opportunities
- Entrepreneurial opportunities
- Added value
- A chance to rebuild their lives
- Improved mindset
- Asset to the society

- etc.

3.4 To Government:

- Opportunities for increased tax
- Easier society to manage
- Added value to the society
- Reduced crime rate (especially for reoffending)
- etc.

4. Business Name and URL

If you're going to have a business or a business website or maybe a social media platform, you need to think about the name of the business, and the name of the URL or the name of your social media platform, etc.

Here are some of the things to consider:

- A concise name
- Easy to remember (this could be a word or a short phrase).
- It should be relevant to your value offer.
- For the purpose of this business, suggestions your business name are:

- *2nd Chance*
- *Another Chance*

- In the case of a website, you could consider:

- 2ndchance.com

- anotherchance.com
- anotherchance.net
- anotherchance.co.uk
- etc.

5. Business Registration and Ownership

- This could be as a sole proprietor
- A limited liability company
- Joint Venture
- Etc.

- Please, research your options online and choose the one that suits you.

- Good practice is to start small and then to grow big.
- Also, you need to understand that each business type has its pros and cons, hence, it's up to you to make a judgement call as to whether or not you would change the business name or model sooner or later.

6. Could I collaborate?

Yes, you could collaborate with like minds. You could share resources in cash and in kind. You could brainstorm together. You could leverage the <u>Profit Sharing Formula App</u> to share profits, ethically, efficiently and fairly. You could also leverage each other.

7. Digital Footprints

As you probably know, we're in a digital world. This could add value to what you do. You could leverage:
- *Websites*
- *Blogs*
- *Podcasts*
- *Social Media*
- *E-books*
- *Membership sites*
- *Etc.*

- These could help with your marketing efforts, and could act as platforms for you to share your value proposition.

8. Marketing Plan

You could do the marketing yourself, or outsource it to freelance professionals. Potential marketing platforms are:

- Social media
- Podcast
- Google
- Bing
- WhatsApp
- Telegram
- YouTube
- Facebook
- LinkedIn
- Influencers
- Tik Tok
- Etc.

Don't forget that marketing is the soul of every business No matter how good your product or service is, if no one knows about it, it is as good as dead. You need to have a regular marketing budget, and to have the mindset that marketing never stops. You shall continually reinvest in marketing, and hopefully continually optimize your monetization.

You might consider:

- Affiliate marketers
- Social media marketers
- Influencers
- Digital marketers
- TV marketers
- Radio marketers
- Print marketers
- Podcast marketers
- WhatsApp marketers
- Referrals
- Word of mouth
- Search Engine Optimization
- Content marketers
- Email marketers
- Etc.

9. Search Engine Optimization and Keyword Research

As part of your marketing plan, it's good practice to optimize searches on the internet. You need to find out related searches which are being made on the internet and then position similar keywords on your digital platforms so that you could easily be located and so that you could optimize your monetization potential.

10. Niche, Demographics, and Client Avatar

- You need to choose your niche or niches
- You need to decide on your demographics of choice
- The above shall help you direct your content to your client avatar and to have more focused and suitable content
- As the entrepreneurial journey continues, you could market and re-market products and services to them, etc.

11. Format

The format could be in audio, video, text.

12. Mission

At Jack Lookman Limited,

Our mission is to empower and inspire generations by leveraging the internet.

13. Curriculum and Signposts

Create relevant curriculum for your chosen demographics. These could include:

- Housing
- Entrepreneurship
- Income streams
- Tax
- Benefits (especially for those in the United Kingdom and the West).
- Relevant Signposts
- Relationships
- Spirituality
- Mindset
- Information technology
- Culinary skills (and signposts)
- Signposts to platforms such as udemy.com (where they could learn through digital means)
- Signposts to useful courses and content
- Training and development options
- Content creation skills
- Funding opportunities (grants, loans, etc)
- Skills audit
- Passion audit
- Mindfulness
- Networking skills
- Preparing for job, interviews (and relevant signposts)
- Collaboration skills
- Other useful signposts
- Becoming the best version of yourself
- Mentoring and coaching opportunities
- Basic research and development skills
- Resource management

- Time management
- Budgeting skills
- Investment skills
- Money saving tips
- Health and wellbeing
- Business grants
- Job hunting skills
- Signpost for education (this could be formal or informal)
- Social Signposts
- Digital signposts
- Sports and Leisure Signpost
- Religious signpost
- Signposts to Community groups
- Signposts on how to do affiliate marketing
- Becoming organized
- Optimizing social media
- Marital tips
- Tips on bringing up children
- Managing bereavement
- Managing ill-health
- Health lifestyle
- Etc.

You could either curate the content, collaborate with others or signpost accordingly, or maybe do a combination of the aforementioned.

14. Disclaimer and Indemnifications

- You need to protect yourself legally. Include disclaimers and indemnifications as necessary.

Hopefully, if there is a call for litigation, you shall be fully or partially protected. You could do this yourself, or get relevant professionals to do so.
You also need to effectively manage expectations between all concerned parties.

- We at Jack Lookman Limited also indemnify ourselves accordingly. This content is merely an idea; it doesn't guarantee any income or wealth.

It takes more than an idea to do so; you need to perfect the idea; you need to dot all i's and cross all t's. You need to carry out due diligence and hopefully monetize, and maybe become rich and wealthy.
- At Jack Lookman Limited, We do Affiliate Marketing by promoting products and services. Upon making sales, we get commissions at no additional cost to you.

15. Target audience

• This shall be those who missed out on formal or informal education at some point or the other.
• And those hoping to rebuild their lives after life-changing experiences
• These could be youths, adults or relevant others.
• This could be in individual countries of choice or globally.

16. Content Creation Implementation

You could create the content yourself or you could collaborate with others. Or you could outsource it. Remember to claim the intellectual rights from the onset and to proactively protect the content. Ensure that you use easily, understandable vocabulary and avoid unnecessary jargon. It's probably good practice to have the content in concise, easy-to-understand modules.

17. Language

• This could be in English or other languages of your target demographics
• You could also create content in multiple languages, if there is a demand for such, and if there is a compelling business case. You could actually outsource the translation as necessary

18. Outsourcing

Sometimes, the workload might be overwhelming or you may not have all the relevant skillsets. In such instances, it may make sense for you to outsource some or all of the work. You may then supervise or project-manage. You will require money to pay the freelancer and the freelance platform. In order to effectively outsource, you need to meticulously spell out your requirement and hire the right freelancers.

Some useful tips are to:

- Check out their reviews
- Ensure they are 4-to-5-star rating
- Ensure they have relevant experience
- Ensure that you could collaborate effectively.
- Ensure that you could afford their service plus the freelance platform's costs.
- Ensure that expectations are fully managed
- Agree on deliverables and milestones
- Check the platforms terms and conditions.
- Arrange an audio or video interview for shortlisted freelancers as necessary
- Agree on payment milestones
- Give a honest review at the end of the process

18.1 Some of the freelancing platforms you may consider are:

- peopleperhour.com
- Fiverr.com
- Freelancer.com
- Upwork.com
- etc.

19. The Value Proposition

- The main product that you shall be offering is a membership site
- It shall contain content in audio, video, text, or a combination
- Users shall pay to access the content
- Payments could be monthly, quarterly, annually, etc.
- There are opportunities for them to communicate with you

- You could additionally include a social media platform such as Facebook for them to intermingle
- There are different membership site providers such as:
    - Member Vault
    - Thinkific
    - Kajabi
    - Podia
    - etc.
- The one I use is Member Vault

- If you require support or setting up a similar platform, please, contact me at <u>Business Collaboration With Jack Lookman</u>
- My Member Vault Website is called 'Jack's Empowerment' the url is <u>jacksempowerment.com</u>

20. Could there be a Sales funnel?

Indeed, there could be a sales funnel. You could have a lead magnet. This could be a free course on your membership site. It could be a free e-book; it could be a free 15 minutes consultation. It could be a social media video, etc. The purpose of the lead magnet is to capture the contact details of potential clients. You could then offer different product and service along the value chain. This could be of equal, higher, or lower value than the main value proposition. For example, in addition to your different product and services, you could offer other related product and service. As part of your marketing plan, you could also signpost clients to other products and services, even if you don't make money on some of these (I guess that this is thinking outside the box).

Your sales funnel could include:

- 1-1 mentoring
- 1-many mentoring
- Other content
- Signposts to affiliate product and services
- Multiple Digital courses
- Physical products
- Etc.

21. Will Payment be one-off or Recurring?

- For membership sites, payments are usually recurring
- Users could pay monthly, quarterly, annually etc; until they no longer require the product or until their pockets run dry. Thereafter or concurrently, new sets of clients could sign up.
- As long as great and useful value is offered, you shall continue to remain in business.

22. Funding Options

For the business this could include investors, crowdfunding, collaborators, sponsors, loans, family and friends, savings, etc.

23. Sponsorships

Sponsorships could be got for the project as well as for the potential clients. For the potential clients, the sponsors could pay the initial amount or for part of the cost; this could be part of corporate social responsibility, which is also known as CSR. Government could also sponsor users; after all, this could add value to the users and to society. It could help to reduce crime and reoffending. It could indirectly add tax earnings in the longterm from the different parties which may include yourself as the entrepreneur. In fact, they could earn tax from the sponsor, from the users (in the short, or long term), from you (the entrepreneur), from others on the value chain, etc.

Some advantages to the sponsors are: advertising potentials and maybe affiliate marketing potentials. You may decide to have one or more sponsors.

24. Income Streams

These could include:
- Membership site/s
- Blog/s
- Paperbacks
- E-books
- One-to-one mentoring
- One-to-many mentoring
- Podcast
- Social media monetization
- Affiliate marketing

- Adverts
- Sponsors
- Collaborations
- Product sales
- Public speaking opportunities
- Sales funnel
- Etc.

25. Prioritization

- You need to prioritize the quickest and most profitable income streams.
- You need to create a business plan.
- You need to articulate the resources required
- You need to seek support and also train as necessary
- You need to carry out due diligence
- You need to think about the return on investment
- You need to think about the return on advertisements and marketing spent
- You need to re-invest as necessary
- You need to scale the business
- You need to involve collaborators as necessary
- You need to leverage different platforms
- You need to keep an eye on the best performing activities and then increase resources
- As well as reduce resources spent on low performing activities

26. Costing and Pricing Considerations

These could include:
- Website hosting
- Website domain names
- Time
- Effort
- Skills
- Human resources
- Marketing
- Profit margin
- Social media management
- Tax
- Administration
- Brainstorming / strategizing
- Fundraising
- Insurance
- IT (information technology)
- competition
- demand and supply
- affordability by target audience
- variable pricing
- leveraging discounts and coupon codes
- Etc.

27. Research and Development

To stand a better chance of success, you need to do your research.

Consider:
- Market research
- Competitor research

- Product research
- Client Avatar research
- Etc.

28. Complimentary Products and Services

- In addition to the membership site
- You could have social media platforms
- You could have blogs, podcasts, paperbacks.
- You could offer mentoring and coaching
- You could do public speaking
- You could collaborate with third parties, etc.

29. Budgetary Considerations

Please see the section under costing and pricing. You could also need to include a factor of safety for unplanned cost, as well as to mitigate any risks. For example, after you've done your budget, you might want to consider multiplying your annual budget by 1.5 or by times 2, and that way you can give allowance for unplanned expenses.

30. Will there be certifications for students?

- In my opinion the certification is not as important as the value received and implemented.
- If users however require a certificate, this could be offered as an extra at additional cost.

- There could be different levels of certification; this could be certificates of attendance or completion and possibly certificates of proficiency
- The certificates could be automatically generated and printed by the user
- There shall be examinations as necessary
- Checks and balances need to be put in place to avoid fraud and malpractice
- Certification shall be done at additional cost
- If you wish to push entrepreneurial limits, the certificate may require updating after about 2 years or 3 years, at additional cost to the user. Please, be mindful of legal and ethical implications of this.

31. What problem are you solving?

- You are basically empowering and inspiring demographics of those who wish to have another chance at optimizing their potential; these could be those who are punished by the law and missed out on education.
- It could be educational dropouts
- It could be those who wish to retrain
- It could be those who missed out on educational opportunities due to life-changing situations; for example war, or earthquakes, etc
- It could be those who couldn't get an education due to poverty
- It could be those who missed out on education due to wrong choices.
- This is about empowering and inspiring those demographics in cost effective ways, such that they

could be of great benefit to themselves and greater benefits to society.

32. Legalities

• You need to consider intellectual rights, non-disclosure agreements, contracts and agreements, General Data Protection Regulation (GDPR in Europe), litigation, insurance, etc.

33. Platforms

Here are suggestions of platforms for your products and services.
You could consider:
• Blogs
• Membership sites
• Social media platforms like YouTube, Facebook, TikTok, LinkedIn, etc
• You could also consider podcasts, apps, paperbacks, ebooks, etc.

34. Risk Management Considerations

• You need to think ahead of potential risks, and mitigate them. For example, there could be conflict within and outside the business
• There could be intellectual rights issues
• Clients may feel short changed

- Expectations may not be fully met within or outside the business
- There may be cancellation and refund issues
- Etc

- The good thing about being aware of potential risks is that they could be effectively mitigated
- It's important to carry out due diligence by spending some time to perfect your value proposition and saving a lot more time later on.

35. Expectation Management

- With business, as in most things in life, there are no guarantees.
- You need to carry out due diligence.
- Cross every *t* and dot every *i*
- You need to consult as necessary with relevant others
- You need to pray for success as well as hope for success.
- You need to have a positive mindset, a mindset which will help you to achieve your aims.

- Even though, this is a good business idea and model, there are no guarantees of a smooth sail.

36. Profit-Sharing Formula

- Mention has been made of collaborators and investors earlier-on; but how could you effectively manage the process?
- How could you effectively, fairly, and ethically share profits and loss?
- How could you be accountable and transparent?
- How could you build trust among stakeholders?

- At Jack Lookman Limited we are working on a <u>Profit Sharing Formula App</u>. This shall hopefully tick most or all of the highlighted challenges. You could learn more about the Profit Sharing Formula App on our different platforms
- You could check on <u>amazon</u>, <u>YouTube</u>, <u>Jack's Empowerment</u>, <u>our blog</u>, etc.

37. Business Plan

There is a great need for a business plan. This shall help you navigate the business process. It shall highlight difficulties and bring to your attention things which you may not have considered. It shall give clarity to the business and add great value to your value proposition. It's good practice to update your business plan regularly.

There's a lot of content on Google and YouTube on how to do a business plan. Alternatively, you could seek professional help; this could however prove to be expensive. Another alternative is to get a stakeholder in the business to complement your skill shortage or probably use a freelancer to do to the business plan.

38. Must All the Content Be Mine?

Well, not really, some of the content could be yours. Some might be of other stakeholders or collaborators; you could signpost clients to useful content or you could share links to blogs and YouTube videos. As long as the client is getting value, all parties remain happy. In addition to this, you could get a freelancer to write the content for you or to create the membership site for you.

39. Is there a need for Feedback Mechanisms?

In my opinion, I think yes, there is. Let's explore some of them:

- You could have questionnaires, feedback tick sheets, feedback with email or text, feedback on social media via likes, shares, subscription, and comments
- You could use survey monkey, or google forms
- Some feedback could be positive, negative or constructive. If handled properly, feedback helps improve the quality of your value proposition
- If handled improperly you could ignore it or become continuously defensive, in such a case you may not focus effectively on what you do, and rather than moving forward you spend your time being reactive.

- There's a small proverb which I learned somewhere along the line, *'if you spend a lifetime looking back, and reacting to barking dogs, you may never move forward, to achieve your life purpose.'*
- So, feedback is very important, but you need to be wise in the way and manner you respond to it. You need to use it constructively and leverage it to achieve positive outcomes.

40. Skills Required for the Business

Some of them include:
- Communication skills
- Entrepreneurial skills
- Content creation skills
- Marketing skills
- People management skills
- Interpersonal skills
- Customer services skills
- IT skills
- Outsourcing skills
- Project management skills
- Troubleshooting skills
- Etc

41. Could the business be automated?

- In my opinion, yes. Once the initial work is done, most of the business could be run on autopilot.
- You may only require maintenance and marketing; and maybe a bit of customer service.

- The maintenance could require updates as necessary
- The marketing could help create a continuous stream clients

42. How much is required to start the business?

- A conservative estimate of about £500.00 or less could do justice to starting the business.

42.1 Some of the key milestones are:
- Creating a membership site
- Creating a business plan
- Doing your business registration
- Creating a social media platform
- Creating the content
- Funding
- Profit Sharing Formula
- Sales funnel
- Administration
- Brainstorming / strategising
- Marketing
- Research and Development
- Involving relevant human resources
- Creating systems and structures
- Etc.

43. Funding

- There are many factors that sustain businesses. Money is just one of them.
- There are other factors such as skills, time, management, marketing, strategizing, etc
- You could contribute what you have either in cash or in kind
- You could collaborate with similar minds
- You could find investors
- You could crowdfund
- You could leverage the Profit Sharing Formula App to fairly, ethically and efficiently share profit and loss,
- In a nutshell your lack of money shouldn't be an impediment for starting the business;

- Also, be mindful of capital and running costs

44. How Soon Could the Business be Up and Running?

With the right resources, the business could be up and running within a month or two. Income could start trickling-in within that period. You could hopefully break-even between six months to one year.

45. How do I go About Starting the Business?

- Luckily, most of the thinking is already done for you.
- You now need to perfect the business idea
- You need to create a team, to reduce cost
- You may involve collaborators and leverage the Profit Sharing Formula App

- You might also leverage Jack Lookman to give greater insight, and to collaborate. Jack Lookman could help build the membership site, social media platforms, marketing, strategizing. Once the strong foundations are built, the maintenance shall be easy.

46. Do I need to be an Expert?

- Well, not really. If you have a good team, you could jointly accomplish the tasks.
- You could leverage each other and share profits accordingly
- You however need to make a contribution of some sort, either in cash or in kind

47. Could Passive Residual Income be Earned from this Business?

Well, firstly we need to clarify that passive income doesn't mean 100% passivity. (I hope there's a word like that). You still need to put in effort from time to time, however the efforts shall be comparatively smaller.

The answer to the question is yes. There's great potential to earn passive residual income. At some point you may need to update your content; at other times you may need to do marketing. In some cases, you may need to do customer service, but generally speaking not as much effort or resource shall be required after the initial chunk of work is executed.

48. Unique Selling Proposition

Is there anything unique about this value proposition? The answer in my opinion is yes.

Even though there are may be bits and pieces of unrelated content in the marketplace, this proposition is unique for the chosen demographic. The content is also specific and in a possibly forgotten niche. The product is unique in the presented form. You could enjoy a monopoly for a while pending the time copy cats come on board.

49. Resources Required for The Business

These include:
- Skills
- Human Resources
- Money
- Digital gadgets
- Digital platforms
- Marketing strategy
- Positive mindset
- Internet connection
- Etc

50. Requirements For the Client

Well, the clients need:
- Basic IT skills
- Communication skills

- Positive mindset
- Willingness to learn and act
- Commitment to learning
- Payment for the resources (or maybe finding sponsors)
- Etc

51. Should the product be Local or Global?

This is a judgment call for you. You need to make various considerations; for example, profitability, language, the niche, the relevance, resources required, competition, affordability, culture, demand, etc.
However, being a digital product, it could easily travel far and wide at little or no additional cost.

52. Process and Project Management

- You need to articulate a plan on how you can transform the idea into a product
- You need to have the relevant resources
- You need to brainstorm and strategize
- You need to have the right personnel to execute
- You may get some things wrong, hence, you need to correct them.
- There might be bottlenecks along the way; you need to navigate these.
- You need to plan for the immediate and long terms
- You need to have plans a, b and c in case either of them fails.

- You also need to bear in mind running costs such as website hosting, domain name, administrative costs, and other business costs.
- To save on costs you may consider using freelancers.

53. Do I Require an Office for This Business?

In my opinion, you probably do not. You could leverage the internet and your digital devices. You could do your collaborations online. You could use your home as your office.

As the business grows you could consider having an office.

Having an office, and a face to the business could however add credibility to your value proposition.

54. Benefits And Opportunities

- Added societal value
- Individual empowerment and inspiration
- Wealth creation
- Job creation
- Affordable mentoring
- Crime reduction
- Taxable income from users, the business, and 3rd parties.
- Informal education
- Skill enhancement
- User-friendly education
- Affordable education

- Etc.

55. Threats and Weaknesses

- The business affects the status quo
- There could be technical issues
- There could be issues of affordability by the target audience
- There could be non-availability of electricity
- There could be non-availability of telecommunications network
- There could be issues of affordability of digital device and telecommunication data by the potential client
- There could be commitment issues by the client
- There could be payment gateway issues
- There could be copycats
- There could be detractors to the project
- Etc.
-

56. Could the Products and Services become Evergreen?

- Well, that's a possibility, depending on the relevance of your content as well as your audience. Like I mentioned earlier, you need to carry out maintenance work as necessary.
- Some of your content may be relevant in years to come, while some may become obsolete. It's for you to manage your content, so that the tides of time can still find them relevant. However, there have been

some evergreen subjects which time might not have overtaken; things like business, arithmetic, language, spirituality, entrepreneurship, etc.
- You need to position yourself accordingly.
- The good news however, is that the digital content you provide is very flexible and dynamic, hence you could modify it to suit the times.

- To answer the question, most of your content could be evergreen and beneficial to generations; but there are many courses in the marketplace to compete against.

- In my opinion, there's a lot of disjointed content in the marketplace for our content avatar; however, our content shall be niche-specific.

- Another point to note is that it doesn't matter if there are many individual courses in the marketplace; as long as we've carried out our due diligence, and there's a space in the marketplace for us, then we are in business.

- We could then focus on our clients and growth; and work on making them lifetime clients who could introduce similar others.

57. Monetization Plan

Some thoughts for monetization are:

- Effective Marketing
- Sales funnel
- Reinvestment
- Great value proposition
- Relevant content
- Collaborations
- Multiple products and services
- Sponsors
- Adverts
- Affiliate Marketing
- Email marketing
- Affordability
- Different payment plans: for example monthly, quarterly or annual payments.
- Different payment gateways: for example; PayPal, Stripe, Payoneer, Flutterwave, etc.
- Multiple language options (translations)
- User-friendly products and services
- Effectively leveraging your users for re-marketing and multiple purchases. They could also spread the word to their network and purchase your other products and services
- You could include Affiliate Marketing options, so that interested Affiliate Marketers could monetise
- You shall also make your value proposition very attractive
- You could also leverage e-mail marketing after you've captured the contact details of your clients and other relevant interested parties.
- Be mindful of legal constraints

58. Value

Upon consuming this content.
- Did you get value?
- Were your thoughts stimulated?
- Did you think about different dimensions to the business?
- Will you consider pursuing the business?
- Will you consider pursuing a different business?
- Will you consider reading and listening to other topics in our series ' <u>Jack's Curated Business Ideas</u>?'
- Would you like to share your thoughts?
- Will you consider collaborating with Jack Lookman?
- Will you consider being mentored by Jack Lookman?
- Will you consider purchasing the book?
- Will you consider gifting the book?
- Will you consider sharing the blog?
- Will you consider investing in the Jack Lookman brand?
- Will you consider investing in any of our selected products and services?
- Will you consider Business Collaboration With Jack Lookman?
- Are you passionate about making impact?

- Whatever be the case, please consider visiting our content; we have:
  - blogs
  - social media platforms
  - paperbacks
  - e-books

- membership site
- app
- etc

Visit jacklookmanlimited.com to get signposted accordingly.

There are mentoring, investment and collaboration opportunities at Jack Lookman Limited. Please browse through our various content and if you resonate with our value offerings and wish to collaborate, please contact us via 'Business Collaboration With Jack Lookman' or via 'Jack's Mentoring 101' or email us at: info@jacklookmanlimited.com

- We could collaborate on our curated business ideas
- We could also collaborate on content creation
- We also offer mentoring and coaching where we could share knowledge and experiences on what we do.

- This is Jack Lookman signing off.

- Ire o (I wish you blessings)
- Ire Kabiti (I wish you great blessings).

Thank you to John Tosin Adekunle for your contribution.

A. Useful links:

Profit Sharing Formula App - short Youtube video

Profit Sharing Formula App - long Youtube video

Profit Sharing Formula App - blog - curatedbusinessideas.com

Profit Sharing Formula App - book

Watch The Youtube Video

Watch and Subscribe to our Youtube channel - Curated Business Ideas

Facebook group - Curated Business Ideas

Facebook Community - Jack Lookman

Jack Lookman Limited Websites - jacklookmanlimited.com

Jack Lookman Limited Paperbacks - jacklookmanlimited.com

Jaaloo Puzzles - jaaloopuzzles.com

Jaaloo Puzzles Tutorial - jaaloopuzzles.com

Business Collaboration With Jack Lookman (18+) - jacksempowerment.com

Jack's Mentoring 101 (18+) - jacksempowerment.com

Becoming Organised - jacksempowerment.com

Jack Lookman's Social Media - jacklookmanlimited.com

Jack's Curated Business Ideas - jacksempowerment.com

B. About JACK LOOKMAN

Olayinka Carew, aka Jack Lookman is the 1st of 5 Children.

He has 3 children, and elderly mum. He is resident in the United Kingdom and is of Nigerian origin.

He studied at King's College, Lagos and University of Lagos.

He has varied life and work experiences.

He has been involved in voluntary and paid jobs.

He is dedicating the rest of his life to empowering and inspiring generations.

This is one of his legacy projects.

Though he has health challenges, he does not let that halt his mission and vision.

Even though he studied Engineering in University; his calling is so many miles away from that. He is currently a Content Creator, Entrepreneur, Collaborative App Developer, Volunteer and Mentor. He is the Director and Owner of Jack Lookman Limited, a registered business in the United Kingdom and their aim is to empower and inspire generations by leveraging the internet.

jacklookmanlimited.com
info@jacklookmanlimited.com
curatedbusinessideas.com

C. Important Notice:

At Jack Lookman Limited there are opportunities for investors and collaborators.

D. Feedback

Please forward your feedback to info@jacklookmanlimited.com

E. Signposts:

Jack Lookman's Websites - jacklookmanlimited.com

Jack Lookman Limited - jacklookmanlimited.com

Jack Lookman On Social Media - jacklookmanlimited.com

Business Collaboration With Jack Lookman - jacksempowerment.com

Jack's Mentoring 101 - jacksempowerment.com

Book A Chat With Jack Lookman - jacksempowerment.com

Jack Lookman's Paperbacks - jacklookmanlimited.com

Jack Lookman's Ebooks - selar.co

Becoming Organised - jacksempowerment.com

Affiliate Marketing Course - jacksempowerment.com

Jaaloo Puzzles - Instructions - jaaloopuzzles.com

Jaaloo Puzzles - Access - games.skillz.com

Baby Jaaloo Puzzles - jaaloo.com

Jack's Curated Business Ideas - jacksempowerment.com

Yoruba Project - yorubaproject.com

F. Disclaimer

We are also affiliate marketers. We promote products and services of ourselves and third parties and get monetized at no additional cost to you.

G. Mission

Our mission at Jack Lookman Limited is to empower and Inspire Generations by leveraging the internet.

H. Did you get value?

We hope that you got some value from this content, learnt 1 or 2 things, and that it stimulated your thoughts; if so, please consider sharing with others as well as sharing your comments.

If interested in collaborations, you could send a short email to info@jacklookmanlimited.com and we shall respond.

You could also 'Book A Chat With Jack Lookman' at jacksempowerment.com

We've also written many books. Please search for Jack Lookman's books on the internet, or visit jacklookmanlimited.com

- You could also join Jack Lookman's community on Facebook. Search for Jack Lookman on Facebook

- We Create Content
- We Mentor
- We do Affiliate Marketing
- We do Business Collaborations
- And App Development Collaborations

- We've authored and published several books on
  - Curated Business Ideas
  - Mindset
  - Poetry
  - Jaaloo Puzzles
  - Yoruba
  - Life Experience
  - Etc

- If you are interested in playing an arithmetic number game called Jaaloo Puzzles, it's very good brain exercise for children, adults, youths and the elderly. It helps with accuracy skills, mental alertness, competition skills, arithmetic and logic skills. You could find it at jaaloo.com and jaaloopuzzles.com

- Are you interested in Business Collaboration With Jack Lookman ?
- Or in Jack's Mentoring 101 ?
- If yes, search for it or them at jacksempowerment.com

I. Useful compliments

1. Jack's Empowerment - membership site - jacksempowerment.com
2. Jaaloo Puzzles - blog - jaaloopuzzles.com - jaaloo.com
3. Curated Business Ideas - blog - curatedbusinessideas.com
4. Jack Lookman Limited - blog - jacklookmanlimited.com
5. Youtube channel: Curated Business Ideas
6. Youtube channel: Jaaloo Puzzles
7. Youtube channel: Life Lessons For Teenagers
8. Facebook: Jack Lookman
9. Facebook: Curated Business Ideas
10. Facebook: Jaaloo Puzzles
11. Facebook: Life Lessons For Teenagers
12. Jack Lookman's Books - jacklookmanlimited.com
13. Business Collaboration With Jack Lookman - jacksempowerment.com
14. Jack's Mentoring 101 - jacksempowerment.com
15. Life Lessons For Teenagers : lifelessonsforteenagers.com
16. Book A Chat With Jack Lookman : jacksempowerment.com
17. TikTok - jacklookman4
18. LinkedIn - Olayinka Carew aka Jack Lookman
19. Yoruba Project - yorubaproject.com

J. Useful hashtags

1. #jackscuratedbusinessidea
2. #jackscuratedbusinessideas
3. #JaalooPuzzles
4. #CuratedBusinessIdeas
5. #JackLookmanLimited
6. #ireo
7. #Irekabiti
8. #JackLookman
9. #empoweringandinspiringgenerations
10. #EmpowermentandInspiration
11. #YorubaProject
12. #oweYoruba
13. #edeYoruba
14. #AdebanjiOsanyingbemi
15. #OlayinkaCarew

K. Books by Jack Lookman

Visit:

- jacklookmanlimited.com
- Internet search - Jack Lookman
- Jack Lookman's Books
- amazon.co.uk

- reputable book shops (online)

L. Some resources by Jack Lookman

- Jack's Empowerment - jacksempowerment.com
- Jaaloo Puzzles - jaaloopuzzles.com
- Jaaloo Puzzles - Baby Jaaloo - jaaloo.com
- Jaaloo Puzzles - jaaloopuzzles.com
- Jack Lookman Limited: jacklookmanlimited.com
- Curated Business Ideas curatedbusinessideas.com
- Life Lessons For Teenagers : lifelessonsforteenagers.com
- Youtube channel: Curated Business Ideas
- Youtube channel: Life Lessons For Teenagers
- Youtube channel: Oro Ishiti- Indelible Yoruba Words
- Youtube channel: Jaaloo Puzzles
- Facebook: Jack Lookman
- Facebook group: Curated Business Ideas
- Facebook group: Menteero
- Facebook group: Jaaloo Puzzles
- Facebook group: Life Lessons For Teenagers
- Facebook group: Oro Ishiti- Indelible Yoruba Words
- Yoruba Project: yorubaproject.com
- Jack's Curated Business Ideas: jacksempowerment.com
- Affiliate Marketing: jacksempowerment.com

- Etc.

M. Will you like to collaborate?

Does the Jack Lookman brand resonate with you? Will you like to collaborate? If yes, please send an email to: info@jacklookmanlimited.com

Use an appropriate subject heading and narrative.

Or search for 'Business Collaboration With Jack Lookman' online.

N. Will you like to be mentored by Jack Lookman?

If yes, please send an email to: info@jacklookmanlimited.com

Use an appropriate subject heading and narrative.

Or search for 'Jack's Mentoring 101' online

O. OTHER PUBLICATIONS BY Jack Lookman Limited

1. *Despair, Submission, Faith and Hope – Volume 1*
2. *Despair, Submission, Faith and Hope – Volume 2*
3. *Monetising Digital Book Reviews*
4. *E-Commerce For Traditional African Attires*
5. *Basic Management And Fundraising Tip For Community Groups*
6. *Monetising A Digital Library*
7. *Ajo, The App And Opportunities*
8. *Empowering Orphans, Widows and Widowers*

9. Submission, Gratitude, Faith and Hope

10. Oro Ishiti- Indelible Yoruba Words - Adebanji Osanyingbemi

11. Eid Monetisation by Leveraging Technology

12. What are your thoughts? What is your mindset? - Volume 1

13. What are your thoughts? What is your mindset? - Volume 2

14. Twenty Curated Business Ideas - Volume 1

15. Jaaloo Puzzles - Volume 1

16. Jaaloo Puzzles - Volume 2

17. Beauty Of The Storm - Gabriel Adeola

18. Digital Career Guidance App

19. Bath Sponge Project

20. Community Group Monetisation

21. Profit Sharing Formula App

22. Event Discount App

23. Leasing Digital Tablets / Gadgets To Undergraduates

24. Monetising Jollof Rice

25. Monetising And Empowering The Nigerian Driver

26. Business Idea Critique

27. Remarkable Lessons From Mothers-In-Law - Jumoke Carew

28. Monetising Life Experience

29. Empowering The Less Educated

30. The Bachelors' Club

31. Could You Create Online Schools?

32. I Wish To Give Sadaqah (Charity), But I'm Broke

33. 352 Yoruba Proverbs Sayings And Translations - Yoruba Project

This is Jack Lookman signing off.

Ire o (I wish you blessings)

Ire kabiti (I wish you loads of blessings).

www.ingramcontent.com/pod-product-compliance
Lightning Source LLC
Chambersburg PA
CBHW050019230526
45470CB00003B/1040